AF654732

The Westminster Confession of Faith

by The Assembly of Divines

Reformed Books

The Westminster Confession of Faith

by the Assembly of Divines

This edition is based on the original 1646 edition, agreed upon by the Assembly of Divines at Westminster.

First edition 2023

ISBN: 978-81-960763-1-3

Cover Design by Dorcas Koshy

© Copyright Gethsemane Media Pvt. Ltd. 2023

All rights reserved. No part of this publication nor cover design may be reproduced without prior permission of the publisher.

Published by

Reformed Books

Reformed Books is an imprint of Gethsemane Media Pvt. Ltd.

For additional Reformed literature in India, contact us.

48-16-11A, Srinagar, Asilmetta Junction, Visakhapatnam 530016, Andhra Pradesh

https://reformedbooks.org

Contents

1
Of the Holy Scripture

1 Although the light of nature and the works of creation and providence do so far manifest the goodness, wisdom, and power of God, as to leave men unexcusable;[a] yet are they not sufficient to give that knowledge of God, and of His will, which is necessary unto salvation.[b] Therefore it pleased the Lord, at sundry times, and in divers manners, to reveal Himself, and to declare His will unto His Church;[c] and afterwards, for the better preserving and propagating of the truth, and for the more sure establishment and comfort of the Church against the corruption of the flesh, and the malice of Satan and of the world, to commit the same wholly unto writing:[d] which maketh the Holy Scripture to be most necessary;[e] those former ways of God's revealing His will unto His people being now ceased.[f]

[a] *Rom 2:14-15; Rom 1:19-20; Ps 19:1-3; Rom 1:32 with Rom 2:1.*
[b] *1 Cor 1:21; 1 Cor 2:13-14.*
[c] *Heb 1:1.*
[d] *Prov 22:19-21; Luke 1:3-4; Rom 15:4; Matt 4:4,7,10; Isa 8:19-20.*
[e] *2 Tim 3:15; 2 Pet 1:19.*
[f] *Heb 1:1-2.*

2 Under the name of Holy Scripture, or the Word of God written, are now contained all the books of the Old and New Testaments, which are these:

Of the Old Testament

Genesis
Exodus
Leviticus
Numbers
Deuteronomy
Joshua
Judges
Ruth
I Samuel
II Samuel
I Kings
II Kings
I Chronicles
II Chronicles
Ezra
Nehemiah
Esther
Job
Psalms
Proverbs
Ecclesiastes
The Song of Songs
Isaiah
Jeremiah
Lamentations
Ezekiel
Daniel
Hosea
Joel
Amos
Obadiah
Jonah
Micah
Nahum
Habakkuk
Zephaniah
Haggai
Zechariah
Malachi

Of the New Testament

The Gospels, according to
Matthew
Mark
Luke
John
The Acts of the Apostles
Paul's Epistles, to the
Romans
Corinthians I
Corinthians II
Galatians
Ephesians
Philippians
Colossians
Thessalonians I
Thessalonians II
To Timothy I
To Timothy II
To Titus
To Philemon
The Epistle to the Hebrews
The Epistle of James
The first and second Epistles of Peter
The first, second, and third Epistles of John
The Epistle of Jude
The Revelation of John

All which are given by inspiration of God, to be the rule of faith and life.[g]

[g] Luke 16:29,31; Eph 2:20; Rev 22:18-19; 2 Tim 3:16.

3 The books commonly called Apocrypha, not being of divine inspiration, are no part of the canon of the Scripture; and therefore are of no authority in the Church of God, nor to be any otherwise approved, or made use of, than other human writings.[h]

[h] Luke 24:27,44; Rom 3:2; 2 Pet 1:21.

4 The authority of the Holy Scripture, for which it ought to be believed and obeyed, dependeth not upon the testimony of any man, or Church; but wholly upon God (who is truth itself) the author thereof: and therefore it is to be received because it is the Word of God.[i]

[i] 2 Pet 1:19,21; 2 Tim 3:16; 1 John 5:9; 1 Thess 2:13.

5 We may be moved and induced by the testimony of the Church to a high and reverent esteem of the Holy Scripture.[k] And the heavenliness of the matter, the efficacy of the doctrine, the majesty of the style, the consent of all the parts, the scope of the whole (which is, to give all glory to God), the full discovery it makes of the only way of man's salvation, the many other incomparable excellencies, and the entire perfection thereof, are arguments whereby it doth abundantly evidence itself to be the Word of God: yet notwithstanding, our full persuasion and assurance of the infallible truth and divine authority thereof, is from the inward work of the Holy Spirit bearing witness by and with the Word in our hearts.[l]

[k] 1 Tim 3:15.

[l] 1 John 2:20,27; John 16:13-14; 1 Cor 2:10-12; Isa 59:21.

6 The whole counsel of God concerning all things necessary for His own glory, man's salvation, faith, and life, is either expressly set down in Scripture, or by good and necessary consequence may be deduced from Scripture: unto which nothing at any time is to be added, whether by new revelations of the Spirit, or traditions of men.[m] Nevertheless we acknowledge the inward illumination of the Spirit of God to be necessary for the saving understanding of such things as are revealed in the Word:[n] and that there are some circumstances concerning the worship of God, and government of the Church, common to human actions and societies, which are to be ordered by the light of nature and Christian prudence, according to the general rules of the Word, which are always to be observed.[o]

[m] 2 Tim 3:15-17; Gal 1:8-9; 2 Thess 2:2.
[n] John 6:45; 1 Cor 2:9-12.
[o] 1 Cor 11:13-14; 1 Cor 14:26,40.

7 All things in Scripture are not alike plain in themselves, nor alike clear unto all:[p] yet those things which are necessary to be known, believed, and observed for salvation, are so clearly propounded and opened in some place of Scripture or other, that not only the learned, but the unlearned, in a due use of the ordinary means, may attain unto a sufficient understanding of them.[q]

[p] 2 Pet 3:16.
[q] Ps 119:105,130.

8 The Old Testament in Hebrew which was the native language of the people of God of old), and the New Testament in Greek (which at the time of the writing of it was most generally known to the nations), being immediately inspired by God, and by His singular care and providence

kept pure in all ages, are therefore authentical;[r] so as, in all controversies of religion, the Church is finally to appeal unto them.[s] But, because these original tongues are not known to all the people of God, who have right unto, and interest in the Scriptures, and are commanded, in the fear of God, to read and search them,[t] therefore they are to be translated into the vulgar language of every nation unto which they come,[u] that the Word of God dwelling plentifully in all, they may worship Him in an acceptable manner;[w] and, through patience and comfort of the Scriptures, may have hope.[x]

[r] Matt 5:18.

[s] Isa 8:20; Acts 15:15; John 5:39,46.

[t] John 5:39.

[u] 1 Cor 14:6,9,11-12, 24,27-28.

[w] Col 3:16.

[x] Rom 15:4.

9 The infallible rule of interpretation of Scripture is the Scripture itself: and therefore, when there is a question about the true and full sense of any Scripture (which is not manifold, but one) it must be searched and known by other places that speak more clearly.[y]

[y] 2 Pet 1:20-21; Acts 15:15-16.

10 The supreme judge by which all controversies of religion are to be determined, and all decrees of councils, opinions of ancient writers, doctrines of men, and private spirits, are to be examined; and in whose sentence we are to rest; can be no other but the Holy Spirit speaking in the Scripture.[z]

[z] Matt 22:29,31; Eph 2:20 with Acts 28:25.

2

Of God, and of the Holy Trinity

1 There is but one only,[a] living, and true God:[b] who is infinite in being and perfection,[c] a most pure spirit,[d] invisible,[e] without body, parts,[f] or passions,[g] immutable,[h] immense,[i] eternal,[k] incomprehensible,[l] almighty,[m] most wise,[n] most holy,[o] most free,[p] most absolute,[q] working all things according to the counsel of His own immutable and most righteous will,[r] for His own glory;[s] most loving,[t] gracious, merciful, long-suffering, abundant in goodness and truth, forgiving iniquity, transgression, and sin;[u] the rewarder of them that diligently seek Him;[w] and withal, most just and terrible in His judgments,[x] hating all sin,[y] and who will by no means clear the guilty.[z]

[a]Deut 6:4; 1 Cor 8:4,6. [b]1 Thess 1:9; Jer 10:10. [c]Job 11:7-9; Job 26:14. [d]John 4:24. [e]1 Tim 1:17. [f]Deut 4:15-16; John 4:24 with Luke 24:39. [g]Acts 14:11,15. [h]James 1:17; Mal 3:6. [i]1 Kings 8:27; Jer 23:23-24. [k]Ps 90:2; 1 Tim 1:17. [l]Ps 145:3. [m]Gen 17:1; Rev 4:8. [n]Rom 16:27. [o]Isa 6:3; Rev 4:8. [p]Ps 115:3. [q]Exod 3:14. [r]Eph 1:11. [s]Prov 16:4; Rom 11:36. [t]1 John 4:8,16. [u]Exod 34:6-7. [w]Heb 11:6. [x]Neh 9:32-33. [y]Ps 5:5-6. [z]Nah 1:2-3; Exod 34:7.

2 God hath all life,[a] glory,[b] goodness,[c] blessedness,[d] in and of Himself; and is alone in and unto Himself all-sufficient, not standing in need of any creatures which He hath made,[e] nor deriving any glory from them,[f] but only manifesting His own glory in, by, unto, and upon them: He is the alone fountain of all being, of whom, through whom, and to whom are all things;[g] and hath most sovereign dominion over them, to do by them, for them, or upon them whatsoever Himself pleaseth.[h] In His sight all things are open and

[a]John 5:26. [b]Acts 7:2. [c]Ps 119:68. [d]1 Tim 6:15; Rom 9:5. [e]Acts 17:24-25. [f]Job 22:2-3. [g]Rom 11:36. [h]Rev 4:11; 1 Tim 6:15; Dan 4:25,35.

manifest;[i] His knowledge is infinite, infallible, and independent upon the creature,[k] so as nothing is to Him contingent, or uncertain.[l] He is most holy in all His counsels, in all His works, and in all His commands.[m] To Him is due from angels and men, and every other creature, whatsoever worship, service, or obedience He is pleased to require of them.[n]

[i]*Heb 4:13.*
[k]*Rom 11:33-34; Ps 147:5.*
[l]*Acts 15:18; Ezek 11:5.*
[m]*Ps 145:17; Rom 7:12.*
[n]*Rev 5:12-14.*

3 In the unity of the Godhead, there be three persons, of one substance, power, and eternity: God the Father, God the Son, and God the Holy Ghost.[o] The Father is of none, neither begotten, nor proceeding: the Son is eternally begotten of the Father:[p] the Holy Ghost eternally proceeding from the Father and the Son.[q]

[o]*1 John 5:7; Matt 3:16-17; Matt 28:19; 2 Cor 13:14.*
[p]*John 1:14,18.*
[q]*John 15:26; Gal 4:6.*

3

Of God's Eternal Decree

1 God, from all eternity did, by the most wise and holy counsel of His own will, freely, and unchangeably ordain whatsoever comes to pass:[a] yet so, as thereby neither is God the author of sin,[b] nor is violence offered to the will of the creatures, nor is the liberty or contingency of second causes taken away, but rather established.[c]

[a] Eph 1:11; Rom 11:33; Heb 6:17; Rom 9:15,18.
[b] James 1:13,17; 1 John 1:5.
[c] Acts 2:23; Matt 17:12; Acts 4:27-28; John 19:11; Prov 16:33.

2 Although God knows whatsoever may or can come to pass upon all supposed conditions,[d] yet hath He not decreed anything because He foresaw it as future, or as that which would come to pass upon such conditions.[e]

[d] Acts 15:18; 1 Sam 23:11-12; Matt 11:21,23.
[e] Rom 9:11,13,16,18.

3 By the decree of God, for the manifestation of His glory, some men and angels[f] are predestinated unto everlasting life, and others foreordained to everlasting death.[g]

[f] 1 Tim 5:21; Matt 25:41.
[g] Rom 9:22-23; Eph 1:5-6; Prov 16:4.

4 These angels and men, thus predestinated and foreordained, are particularly and unchangeably designed, and their number is so certain and definite, that it cannot be either increased or diminished.[h]

[h] 2 Tim 2:19; John 13:18.

5 Those of mankind that are predestinated unto life, God, before the foundation of the world was laid, according to His eternal and immutable purpose, and the secret counsel and good pleasure of His will, hath chosen, in Christ, unto

everlasting glory,[i] out of His mere free grace and love, without any foresight of faith or good works, or perseverance in either of them, or any other thing in the creature, as conditions, or causes moving Him thereunto:[k] and all to the praise of His glorious grace.[l]

[i] *Eph 1:4,9,11; Rom 8:30; 2 Tim 1:9; 1 Thess 5:9.*
[k] *Rom 9:11,13,16; Eph 1:4,9.*
[l] *Eph 1:6,12.*

6 As God hath appointed the elect unto glory, so hath He, by the eternal and most free purpose of His will, foreordained all the means thereunto.[m] Wherefore they who are elected, being fallen in Adam, are redeemed by Christ,[n] are effectually called unto faith in Christ by His Spirit working in due season, are justified, adopted, sanctified,[o] and kept by His power through faith unto salvation.[p] Neither are any other redeemed by Christ, effectually called, justified, adopted, sanctified, and saved, but the elect only.[q]

[m] *1 Pet 1:2; Eph 1:4-5; Eph 2:10; 2 Thess 2:13.*
[n] *1 Thess 5:9,10; Tit 2:14.*
[o] *Rom 8:30; Eph 1:5; 2 Thess 2:13.*
[p] *1 Pet 1:5;*
[q] *John 17:9; Rom 8:28-39; John 6:64-65; John 10:26; John 8:47; 1 John 2:19.*

7 The rest of mankind God was pleased, according to the unsearchable counsel of His own will, whereby He extendeth or withholdeth mercy, as He pleaseth, for the glory of His sovereign power over His creatures, to pass by; and to ordain them to dishonour and wrath, for their sin, to the praise of His glorious justice.[r]

[r] *Matt 11:25-26; Rom 9:17-18,21-22; 2 Tim 2:19-20; Jude 4; 1 Pet 2:8.*

8 The doctrine of this high mystery of predestination is to be handled with special prudence and care,[s] that men attending the will of God revealed in His Word, and yielding obedience thereunto, may, from the certainty of their effectual vocation, be assured of their eternal election.[t] So shall this doctrine afford matter of praise, reverence, and

[s] *Rom 9:20; Rom 11:33; Deut 29:29.*
[t] *2 Pet 1:10.*

[u] Eph 1:6; Rom 11:33. [w] Rom 11:5-6,20; 2 Pet 1:10; Rom 8:33; Luke 10:20.

admiration of God,[u] and of humility, diligence, and abundant consolation to all that sincerely obey the Gospel.[w]

4

Of Creation

1 It pleased God the Father, Son, and Holy Ghost,[a] for the manifestation of the glory of His eternal power, wisdom, and goodness,[b] in the beginning, to create, or make of nothing, the world, and all things therein whether visible or invisible, in the space of six days; and all very good.[c]

[a] *Heb 1:2; John 1:2-3; Gen 1:2; Job 26:13; Job 33:4.* [b] *Rom 1:20; Jer 10:12; Ps 104:24; Ps 33:5-6.* [c] *Gen chap 1; Heb 11:3; Col 1:16; Acts 17:24.*

2 After God had made all other creatures, He created man, male and female,[d] with reasonable and immortal souls,[e] endued with knowledge, righteousness, and true holiness, after His own image;[f] having the law of God written in their hearts,[g] and power to fulfil it:[h] and yet under a possibility of transgressing, being left to the liberty of their own will, which was subject unto change.[i] Beside this law written in their hearts, they received a command, not to eat of the tree of the knowledge of good and evil, which while they kept, they were happy in their communion with God,[k] and had dominion over the creatures.[l]

[d] *Gen 1:27.* [e] *Gen 2:7 with Eccl 12:7 and Luke 23:43 and Matt 10:28.* [f] *Gen 1:26; Col 3:10; Eph 4:24.* [g] *Rom 2:14-15.* [h] *Eccl 7:29.* [i] *Gen 3:6; Eccl 7:29.* [k] *Gen 2:17; Gen 3:8-11,23.* [l] *Gen 1:26,28.*

5
Of Providence

1 God the great Creator of all things doth uphold,[a] direct, dispose, and govern all creatures, actions, and things,[b] from the greatest even to the least,[c] by His most wise and holy providence,[d] according to His infallible foreknowledge,[e] and the free and immutable counsel of His own will,[f] to the praise of the glory of His wisdom, power, justice, goodness, and mercy.[g]

2 Although, in relation to the foreknowledge and decree of God, the first Cause, all things come to pass immutably, and infallibly:[h] yet, by the same providence, He ordereth them to fall out, according to the nature of second causes, either necessarily, freely, or contingently.[i]

3 God, in His ordinary providence maketh use of means,[k] yet is free to work without,[l] above,[m] and against them at His pleasure.[n]

4 The almighty power, unsearchable wisdom, and infinite goodness of God so far manifest themselves in His providence, that it extendeth itself even to the first fall, and all other sins of angels and men;[o] and that not by a bare permission,[p] but such as hath joined with it a most wise and powerful bounding,[q] and otherwise ordering and governing of them, in a manifold dispensation, to His own holy ends;[r] yet so, as the sinfulness thereof proceedeth only from the

[a] Heb 1:3. [b] Dan 4:34-35; Ps 135:6; Acts 17:25-26,28; Job chap 38-41. [c] Matt 10:29-31. [d] Prov 15:3; Ps 104:24; Ps 145:17. [e] Acts 15:18; Ps 94:8-11. [f] Eph 1:11; Ps 33:10-11. [g] Isa 63:14; Eph 3:10; Rom 9:17; Gen 45:7; Ps 145:7. [h] Acts 2:23. [i] Gen 8:22; Jer 31:35; Exod 21:13 with Deut 19:5; 1 Kings 22:28,34; Isa 10:6-7. [k] Acts 27:31,44; Isa 55:10-11; Hos 2:21-22. [l] Hos 1:7; Matt 4:4; Job 34:20. [m] Rom 4:19-21. [n] 2 Kings 6:6; Dan 3:27. [o] Rom 11:32-34; 2 Sam 24:1 with 1 Chron 21:1; 1 Kings 22:22-23; 1 Chron 10:4,13-14; 2 Sam 16:10; Acts 2:23; Acts 4:27-28. [p] Acts 14:16. [q] Ps 76:10; 2 Kings 19:28. [r] Gen 50:20; Isa 10:6-7,12.

creature, and not from God, who, being most holy and righteous, neither is, nor can be, the author or approver of sin.[s]

5 The most wise, righteous, and gracious God doth oftentimes leave for a season His own children to manifold temptations, and the corruption of their own hearts, to chastise them for their former sins, or to discover unto them the hidden strength of corruption, and deceitfulness of their hearts, that they may be humbled;[t] and, to raise them to a more close and constant dependence for their support upon Himself, and to make them more watchful against all future occasions of sin, and for sundry other just and holy ends.[u]

6 As for those wicked and ungodly men whom God, as a righteous Judge, for former sins doth blind and harden,[w] from them He not only withholdeth His grace, whereby they might have been enlightened in their understandings, and wrought upon in their hearts;[x] but sometimes also withdraweth the gifts which they had,[y] and exposeth them to such objects as their corruption makes occasions of sin;[z] and, withal, gives them over to their own lusts, the temptations of the world, and the power of Satan:[a] whereby it comes to pass that they harden themselves, even under those means which God useth for the softening of others.[b]

7 As the providence of God doth in general reach to all creatures, so after a most special manner it taketh care of His Church, and disposeth all things to the good thereof.[c]

[s] *James 1:13-14,17; 1 John 2:16; Ps 50:21.*

[t] *2 Chron 32:25-26, 31; 2 Sam 24:1.*

[u] *2 Cor 12:7-9; Ps 73; Ps 77:1-12; Mark 14:66-72 with John 21:15-17.*

[w] *Rom 1:24,26,28; Rom 11:7-8.*

[x] *Deut 29:4.*

[y] *Matt 13:12; Matt 25:29.*

[z] *Deut 2:30; 2 Kings 8:12-13.*

[a] *Ps 81:11-12; 2 Thess 2:10-12.*

[b] *Exod 7:3 with Exod 8:15,32; 2 Cor 2:15-16; Isa 8:14; 1 Pet 2:7-8; Isa 6:9-10 with Acts 28:26-27.*

[c] *1 Tim 4:10; Amos 9:8-9; Rom 8:28; Isa 43:3-5,14.*

6

Of the Fall of Man, of Sin, and of the Punishment thereof

1 Our first parents, being seduced by the subtilty and temptation of Satan, sinned in eating the forbidden fruit.[a] This their sin God was pleased, according to His wise and holy counsel, to permit, having purposed to order it to His own glory.[b]

2 By this sin they fell from their original righteousness and communion with God,[c] and so became dead in sin,[d] and wholly defiled in all the faculties and parts of soul and body.[e]

3 They being the root of all mankind, the guilt of this sin was imputed,[f] and the same death in sin and corrupted nature conveyed to all their posterity descending from them by ordinary generation.[g]

4 From this original corruption, whereby we are utterly indisposed, disabled, and made opposite to all good,[h] and wholly inclined to all evil,[i] do proceed all actual transgressions.[k]

5 This corruption of nature, during this life, doth remain in those that are regenerated;[l] and although it be, through Christ, pardoned, and mortified, yet both itself and all the motions thereof are truly and properly sin.[m]

6 Every sin, both original and actual, being a transgression of the righteous law of God, and contrary thereunto,[n] doth, in its own nature, bring

[a] Gen 3:13; 2 Cor 11:3.
[b] Rom 11:32.
[c] Gen 3:6-8; Eccl 7:29; Rom 3:23.
[d] Gen 2:17; Eph 2:1.
[e] Tit 1:15; Gen 6:5; Jer 17:9; Rom 3:10-18.
[f] Gen 1:27,28 and Gen 2:16-17 and Acts 17:26 with Rom 5:12,15-19 and 1 Cor 15:21-22,49.
[g] Ps 51:5; Gen 5:3; Job 14:4; Job 15:14.
[h] Rom 5:6; Rom 8:7; Rom 7:18; Col 1:21.
[i] Gen 6:5; Gen 8:21; Rom 3:10-12.
[k] James 1:14-15; Eph 2:2-3; Matt 15:19.
[l] 1 John 1:8,10; Rom 7:14,17-18,23; James 3:2; Prov 20:9; Eccl 7:20.
[m] Rom 7:5,7-8,25; Gal 5:17.

guilt upon the sinner,[o] whereby he is bound over to the wrath of God,[p] and curse of the law,[q] and so made subject to death,[r] with all miseries spiritual,[s] temporal,[t] and eternal.[u]

[n] *1 John 3:4.*
[o] *Rom 2:15; Rom 3:9,19.*
[p] *Eph 2:3.*
[q] *Gal 3:10.*
[r] *Rom 6:23.*
[s] *Eph 4:18.*
[t] *Rom 8:20; Lam 3:39.*
[u] *Matt 25:41; 2 Thess 1:9.*

7

Of God's Covenant with Man

1 The distance between God and the creature is so great, that although reasonable creatures do owe obedience unto Him as their Creator, yet they could never have any fruition of Him as their blessedness and reward, but by some voluntary condescension on God's part, which He hath been pleased to express by way of covenant.[a]

[a] *Isa 40:13-17; Job 9:32-33; 1 Sam 2:25; Ps 113:5-6; Ps 100:2-3; Job 22:2-3; Job 35:7-8; Luke 17:10; Acts 17:24-25.*

2 The first covenant made with man was a covenant of works,[b] wherein life was promised to Adam, and in him to his posterity,[c] upon condition of perfect and personal obedience.[d]

[b] *Gal 3:12.* [c] *Rom 10:5; Rom 5:12-20.* [d] *Gen 2:17; Gal 3:10.*

3 Man, by his fall having made himself incapable of life by that covenant, the Lord was pleased to make a second,[e] commonly called the covenant of grace; wherein He freely offereth unto sinners life and salvation by Jesus Christ, requiring of them faith in Him that they may be saved,[f] and promising to give unto all those that are ordained unto life His Holy Spirit, to make them willing and able to believe.[g]

[e] *Gal 3:21; Rom 8:3; Rom 3:20-21; Gen 3:15; Isa 42:6.* [f] *Mark 16:15-16; John 3:16; Rom 10:6,9; Gal 3:11.* [g] *Ezek 36:26-27; John 6:44-45.*

4 This covenant of grace is frequently set forth in Scripture by the name of a Testament, in reference to the death of Jesus Christ the Testator, and to the everlasting inheritance, with all things belonging to it, therein bequeathed.[h]

[h] *Heb 9:15-17; Heb 7:22; Luke 22:20; 1 Cor 11:25.*

5 This covenant was differently administered in the time of the law, and in the time of the gospel:[i] under the law, it was administered by promises, prophecies, sacrifices, circumcision, the paschal lamb, and other types and ordinances delivered to the people of the Jews, all fore-signifying Christ to come;[k] which were, for that time, sufficient and efficacious, through the operation of the Spirit, to instruct and build up the elect in faith in the promised Messiah,[l] by whom they had full remission of sins, and eternal salvation; and is called, the Old Testament.[m]

[i] *2 Cor 3:6-9.*
[k] *Heb chap 8-10; Rom 4:11; Col 2:11-12; 1 Cor 5:7.*
[l] *1 Cor 10:1-4; Heb 11:13; John 8:56.*
[m] *Gal 3:7-9,14.*

6 Under the gospel, when Christ, the substance,[n] was exhibited, the ordinances in which this covenant is dispensed are the preaching of the Word, and the administration of the sacraments of Baptism and the Lord's Supper:[o] which, though fewer in number, and administered with more simplicity, and less outward glory; yet, in them, it is held forth in more fulness, evidence, and spiritual efficacy,[p] to all nations, both Jews and Gentiles;[q] and is called the New Testament.[r] There are not therefore two covenants of grace, differing in substance, but one and the same, under various dispensations.[s]

[n] *Col 2:17.*
[o] *Matt 28:19-20; 1 Cor 11:23-25.*
[p] *Heb 12:22-28; Jer 31:33-34.*
[q] *Matt 28:19; Eph 2:15-19.*
[r] *Luke 22:20.*
[s] *Gal 3:14,16; Rom 3:21-23,30. Ps 32:1 with Rom 4:3,6, 16-17,23-24; Heb 13:8; Acts 15:11.*

8
Of Christ the Mediator

[a]Isa 42:1; 1 Pet 1:19-20; John 3:16; 1 Tim 2:5. [b]Acts 3:22. [c]Heb 5:5-6. [d]Ps 2:6; Luke 1:33. [e]Eph 5:23. [f]Heb 1:2. [g]Acts 17:31. [h]John 17:6; Ps 22:30; Isa 53:10. [i]1 Tim 2:6; Isa 55:4-5; 1 Cor 1:30.

1 It pleased God, in His eternal purpose, to choose and ordain the Lord Jesus, His only begotten Son, to be the Mediator between God and man;[a] the Prophet,[b] Priest,[c] and King,[d] the Head and Saviour of His Church,[e] the Heir of all things,[f] and Judge of the world:[g] unto whom He did from all eternity give a people, to be His seed,[h] and to be by Him in time redeemed, called, justified, sanctified, and glorified.[i]

[k]John 1:1,14; 1 John 5:20; Phil 2:6; Gal 4:4. [l]Heb 2:14,16-17; Heb 4:15. [m]Luke 1:27,31,35; Gal 4:4. [n]Luke 1:35; Col 2:9; Rom 9:5; 1 Peter 3:18; 1 Tim 3:16. [o]Rom 1:3-4; 1 Tim 2:5.

2 The Son of God, the second person in the Trinity, being very and eternal God, of one substance and equal with the Father, did, when the fulness of time was come, take upon Him man's nature,[k] with all the essential properties and common infirmities thereof, yet without sin:[l] being conceived by the power of the Holy Ghost, in the womb of the virgin Mary, of her substance.[m] So that two whole, perfect, and distinct natures, the Godhead and the manhood, were inseparably joined together in one person, without conversion, composition, or confusion.[n] Which person is very God, and very man, yet one Christ, the only Mediator between God and man.[o]

[p]Ps 45:7; John 3:34. [q]Col 2:3.

3 The Lord Jesus, in His human nature thus united to the divine, was sanctified and anointed with the Holy Spirit, above measure,[p] having in Him all the treasures of wisdom and knowledge;[q] in whom it pleased the Father that all fulness should

dwell;[r] to the end that, being holy, harmless, undefiled, and full of grace and truth,[s] He might be thoroughly furnished to execute the office of a mediator and surety.[t] Which office He took not unto Himself, but was thereunto called by His Father,[u] who put all power and judgment into His hand, and gave Him commandment to execute the same.[w]

4 This office the Lord Jesus did most willingly undertake;[x] which that He might discharge, He was made under the law,[y] and did perfectly fulfil it,[z] endured most grievous torments immediately in His soul,[a] and most painful sufferings in His body;[b] was crucified, and died;[c] was buried, and remained under the power of death; yet saw no corruption.[d] On the third day He arose from the dead,[e] with the same body in which He suffered,[f] with which also he ascended into heaven, and there sitteth at the right hand of His Father,[g] making intercession,[h] and shall return to judge men and angels at the end of the world.[i]

5 The Lord Jesus, by His perfect obedience, and sacrifice of Himself, which He, through the eternal Spirit, once offered up unto God, hath fully satisfied the justice of His Father;[k] and purchased, not only reconciliation, but an everlasting inheritance in the kingdom of heaven, for all those whom the Father hath given unto Him.[l]

6 Although the work of redemption was not actually wrought by Christ till after His incarnation, yet the virtue, efficacy, and benefits thereof were

[r] Col 1:19.
[s] Heb 7:26; John 1:14.
[t] Acts 10:38; Heb 12:24; Heb 7:22.
[u] Heb 5:4-5.
[w] John 5:22,27; Matt 28:18; Acts 2:36.
[x] Ps 40:7-8 with Heb 10:5-10; John 10:18; Phil 2:8.
[y] Gal 4:4. *[z] Matt 3:15; Matt 5:17.*
[a] Matt 26:37-38; Luke 22:44; Matt 27:46.
[b] Matt chap 26-27.
[c] Phil 2:8.
[d] Acts 2:23-24,27; Acts 13:37; Rom 6:9.
[e] 1 Cor 15:3-4.
[f] John 20:25,27.
[g] Mark 16:19.
[h] Rom 8:34; Heb 9:24; Heb 7:25.
[i] Rom 14:9-10; Acts 1:11; Acts 10:42; Matt 13:40-42; Jude 6; 2 Pet 2:4.
[k] Rom 5:19; Heb 9:14,16; Heb 10:14; Eph 5:2; Rom 3:25-26.
[l] Dan 9:24,26; Col 1:19-20; Eph 1:11,14; John 17:2; Heb 9:12,15.

communicated unto the elect in all ages successively from the beginning of the world, in and by those promises, types, and sacrifices, wherein He was revealed, and signified to be the seed of the woman which should bruise the serpent's head; and the Lamb slain from the beginning of the world: being yesterday and today the same, and for ever.[m]

[m] Gal 4:4-5; Gen 3:15; Rev 13:8; Heb 13:8.

7 Christ, in the work of mediation, acteth according to both natures, by each nature doing that which is proper to itself:[n] yet, by reason of the unity of the person, that which is proper to one nature, is sometimes in Scripture attributed to the person denominated by the other nature.[o]

[n] Heb 9:14; 1 Pet 3:18.

[o] Acts 20:28; John 3:13; 1 John 3:16.

8 To all those for whom Christ hath purchased redemption, He doth certainly and effectually apply and communicate the same,[p] making intercession for them,[q] and revealing unto them, in and by the Word, the mysteries of salvation,[r] effectually persuading them by His Spirit to believe and obey, and governing their hearts by His Word and Spirit,[s] overcoming all their enemies by His almighty power and wisdom, in such manner, and ways, as are most consonant to His wonderful and unsearchable dispensation.[t]

[p] John 6:37,39; John 10:15-16.

[q] 1 John 2:1-2; Rom 8:34.

[r] John 15:13,15; Eph 1:7-9; John 17:6.

[s] John 14:26; Heb 12:2; 2 Cor 4:13; Rom 8:9,14; Rom 15:18-19; John 17:17.

[t] Ps 110:1; 1 Cor 15:25-26; Mal 4:2-3; Col 2:15.

9
Of Free Will

1 God hath endued the will of man with that natural liberty, that it is neither forced, nor by any absolute necessity of nature determined to good or evil.[a]

[a]Matt 17:12; James 1:14; Deut 30:19.

2 Man, in his state of innocency, had freedom and power to will and to do that which was good, and well pleasing to God;[b] but yet mutably, so that he might fall from it.[c]

[b]Eccl 7:29; Gen 1:26. [c]Gen 2:16-17; Gen 3:6.

3 Man, by his fall into a state of sin, hath wholly lost all ability of will to any spiritual good accompanying salvation:[d] so as, a natural man, being altogether averse from that good,[e] and dead in sin,[f] is not able, by his own strength, to convert himself, or to prepare himself thereunto.[g]

[d]Rom 5:6; Rom 8:7; John 15:5. [e]Rom 3:10,12. [f]Eph 2:1,5; Col 2:13. [g]John 6:44,65; Eph 2:2-5; 1 Cor 2:14; Tit 3:3-5.

4 When God converts a sinner, and translates him into the state of grace, He freeth him from his natural bondage under sin;[h] and, by His grace alone, enables him freely to will and to do that which is spiritually good;[i] yet so, as that by reason of his remaining corruption, he doth not perfectly, nor only, will that which is good, but doth also will that which is evil.[k]

[h]Col 1:13; John 8:34,36. [i]Phil 2:13; Rom 6:18,22. [k]Gal 5:17; Rom 7:15,18-19, 21,23.

5 The will of man is made perfectly and immutably free to good alone, in the state of glory only.[l]

[l]Eph 4:13; Heb 12:23; 1 John 3:2; Jude 24.

10
Of Effectual Calling

[a] Rom 8:30; Rom 11:7; Eph 1:10-11.
[b] 2 Thess 2:13-14; 2 Cor 3:3,6.
[c] Rom 8:2; Eph 2:1-5; 2 Tim 1:9-10.
[d] Acts 26:18; 1 Cor 2:10,12; Eph 1:17-18.
[e] Ezek 36:26.
[f] Ezek 11:19; Phil 2:13; Deut 30:6; Ezek 36:27.
[g] Eph 1:19; John 6:44-45.
[h] Song 1:4; Ps 110:3; John 6:37; Rom 6:16-18.

1 All those whom God hath predestinated unto life, and those only, He is pleased in His appointed and accepted time effectually to call,[a] by His Word and Spirit,[b] out of that state of sin and death, in which they are by nature, to grace and salvation by Jesus Christ;[c] enlightening their minds spiritually and savingly to understand the things of God;[d] taking away their heart of stone, and giving unto them an heart of flesh;[e] renewing their wills, and by His almighty power determining them to that which is good,[f] and effectually drawing them to Jesus Christ:[g] yet so, as they come most freely, being made willing by His grace.[h]

[i] 2 Tim 1:9; Tit 3:4-5; Eph 2:4-5,8-9; Rom 9:11.
[k] 1 Cor 2:14; Rom 8:7; Eph 2:5.
[l] John 6:37; Ezek 36:27; John 5:25.

2 This effectual call is of God's free and special grace alone, not from anything at all foreseen in man,[i] who is altogether passive therein, until being quickened and renewed by the Holy Spirit,[k] he is thereby enabled to answer this call, and to embrace the grace offered and conveyed in it.[l]

[m] Luke 18:15-16 and Acts 2:38-39 and John 3:3,5 and 1 John 5:12 and Rom 8:9 [compared together].
[n] John 3:8.
[o] 1 John 5:12; Acts 4:12.

3 Elect infants, dying in infancy, are regenerated, and saved by Christ through the Spirit,[m] who worketh when, and where, and how He pleaseth:[n] so also are all other elect persons who are uncapable of being outwardly called by the ministry of the Word.[o]

4 Others, not elected, although they may be called by the ministry of the Word,[p] and may have some common operations of the Spirit,[q] yet they never truly come unto Christ, and therefore cannot be saved:[r] much less can men, not professing the Christian religion, be saved in any other way whatsoever, be they never so diligent to frame their lives according to the light of nature, and the law of that religion they do profess.[s] And, to assert and maintain that they may, is very pernicious, and to be detested.[t]

[p] *Matt 22:14.*
[q] *Matt 7:22; Matt 13:20-21; Heb 6:4-5.*
[r] *John 6:64-66; John 8:24.*
[s] *Acts 4:12; John 14:6; Eph 2:12; John 4:22; John 17:3.*
[t] *2 John 9-11; 1 Cor 16:22; Gal 1:6-8.*

11
Of Justification

1 Those whom God effectually calleth, He also freely justifieth:[a] not by infusing righteousness into them, but by pardoning their sins, and by accounting and accepting their persons as righteous; not for anything wrought in them, or done by them, but for Christ's sake alone; nor by imputing faith itself, the act of believing, or any other evangelical obedience to them, as their righteousness, but by imputing the obedience and satisfaction of Christ unto them,[b] they receiving and resting on Him and His righteousness by faith; which faith they have not of themselves, it is the gift of God.[c]

[a] Rom 8:30; Rom 3:24. [b] Rom 4:5-8; 2 Cor 5:19,21; Rom 3:22,24-25, 27-28; Tit 3:5,7; Eph 1:7; Jer 23:6; 1 Cor 1:30,31; Rom 5:17-19. [c] Acts 10:43; Gal 2:16; Phil 3:9; Acts 13:38-39; Eph 2:7-8.

2 Faith, thus receiving and resting on Christ and His righteousness, is the alone instrument of justification;[d] yet it is not alone in the person justified, but is ever accompanied with all other saving graces, and is no dead faith, but worketh by love.[e]

[d] John 1:12; Rom 3:28; Rom 5:1. [e] James 2:17,22,26; Gal 5:6.

3 Christ, by His obedience and death, did fully discharge the debt of all those that are thus justified, and did make a proper, real, and full satisfaction to His Father's justice in their behalf.[f] Yet, inasmuch as He was given by the Father for them;[g] and His obedience and satisfaction accepted in their stead;[h] and both freely, not for anything in them; their justification is only of free grace;[i] that both the exact justice, and rich

[f] Rom 5:8-10,19; 1 Tim 2:5-6; Heb 10:10,14; Dan 9:24,26; Isa 53:4-6,10-12. [g] Rom 8:32. [h] 2 Cor 5:21; Matt 3:17; Eph 5:2. [i] Rom 3:24; Eph 1:7.

grace of God, might be glorified in the justification of sinners.[k]

[k] Rom 3:26; Eph 2:7.

4 God did, from all eternity, decree to justify all the elect,[l] and Christ did, in the fulness of time, die for their sins, and rise again for their justification:[m] nevertheless, they are not justified, until the Holy Spirit doth, in due time, actually apply Christ unto them.[n]

[l] Gal 3:8; 1 Pet 1:2,19-20; Rom 8:30.
[m] Gal 4:4; 1 Tim 2:6; Rom 4:25.
[n] Col 1:21-22; Gal 2:16; Tit 3:3-7.

5 God doth continue to forgive the sins of those that are justified:[o] and, although they can never fall from the state of justification;[p] yet they may, by their sins, fall under God's fatherly displeasure, and not have the light of His countenance restored unto them, until they humble themselves, confess their sins, beg pardon, and renew their faith and repentance.[q]

[o] Matt 6:12; 1 John 1:7,9; 1 John 2:1-2.
[p] Luke 22:32; John 10:28; Heb 10:14.
[q] Ps 89:31-33; Ps 51:7-12; Ps 32:5; Matt 26:75; 1 Cor 11:30,32; Luke 1:20.

6 The justification of believers under the Old Testament was, in all these respects, one and the same with the justification of believers under the New Testament.[r]

[r] Gal 3:9,13-14; Rom 4:22-24; Heb 13:8.

12
Of Adoption

All those that are justified, God vouchsafeth, in and for His only Son Jesus Christ, to make partakers of the grace of adoption,[a] by which they are taken into the number, and enjoy the liberties and privileges of the children of God,[b] have His name put upon them,[c] receive the spirit of adoption,[d] have access to the throne of grace with boldness,[e] are enabled to cry, Abba, Father,[f] are pitied,[g] protected,[h] provided for,[i] and chastened by Him as by a Father;[k] yet never cast off,[l] but sealed to the day of redemption,[m] and inherit the promises,[n] as heirs of everlasting salvation.[o]

[a] *Eph 1:5.*
[b] *Gal 4:4-5; Rom 8:17; John 1:12.*
[c] *Jer 14:9; 2 Cor 6:18; Rev 3:12.*
[d] *Rom 8:15.*
[e] *Eph 3:12; Rom 5:2.*
[f] *Gal 4:6.*
[g] *Ps 103:13.*
[h] *Prov 14:26.*
[i] *Matt 6:30,32; 1 Pet 5:7.*
[k] *Heb 12:6.*
[l] *Lam 3:31.*
[m] *Eph 4:30.*
[n] *Heb 6:12.*
[o] *1 Pet 1:3,4; Heb 1:14.*

13
Of Sanctification

1 They who are effectually called and regenerated, having a new heart and a new spirit created in them, are further sanctified, really and personally, through the virtue of Christ's death and resurrection,[a] by His Word and Spirit dwelling in them:[b] the dominion of the whole body of sin is destroyed,[c] and the several lusts thereof are more and more weakened and mortified;[d] and they more and more quickened and strengthened in all saving graces,[e] to the practice of true holiness, without which no man shall see the Lord.[f]

[a] 1 Cor 6:11; Acts 20:32; Phil 3:10; Rom 6:5-6.
[b] John 17:17; Eph 5:26; 2 Thess 2:13.
[c] Rom 6:6,14.
[d] Gal 5:24; Rom 8:13.
[e] Col 1:11; Eph 3:16-19.
[f] 2 Cor 7:1; Heb 12:14.

2 This sanctification is throughout, in the whole man;[g] yet imperfect in this life, there abiding still some remnants of corruption in every part,[h] whence ariseth a continual and irreconcilable war; the flesh lusting against the Spirit, and the Spirit against the flesh.[i]

[g] 1 Thess 5:23.
[h] 1 John 1:10; Rom 7:18,23; Phil 3:12.
[i] Gal 5:17; 1 Pet 2:11.

3 In which war, although the remaining corruption, for a time, may much prevail;[k] yet through the continual supply of strength from the sanctifying Spirit of Christ, the regenerate part doth overcome;[l] and so, the saints grow in grace,[m] perfecting holiness in the fear of God.[n]

[k] Rom 7:23.
[l] Rom 6:14; 1 John 5:4; Eph 4:15-16.
[m] 2 Pet 3:18; 2 Cor 3:18.
[n] 2 Cor 7:1.

14
Of Saving Faith

[a]Heb 10:39.
[b]2 Cor 4:13; Eph 1:17-19; Eph 2:8.
[c]Rom 10:14,17.
[d]1 Pet 2:2; Acts 20:32; Rom 4:11; Luke 17:5; Rom 1:16-17.

1 The grace of faith, whereby the elect are enabled to believe to the saving of their souls,[a] is the work of the Spirit of Christ in their hearts,[b] and is ordinarily wrought by the ministry of the Word,[c] by which also, and by the administration of the sacraments, and prayer, it is increased and strengthened.[d]

[e]John 4:42; 1 Thess 2:13; 1 John 5:10; Acts 24:14.
[f]Rom 16:26.
[g]Isa 66:2.
[h]Heb 11:13; 1 Tim 4:8.
[i]John 1:12; Acts 16:31; Gal 2:20; Acts 15:11.

2 By this faith, a Christian believeth to be true whatsoever is revealed in the Word, for the authority of God Himself speaking therein;[e] and acteth differently upon that which each particular passage thereof containeth; yielding obedience to the commands,[f] trembling at the threatenings,[g] and embracing the promises of God for this life, and that which is to come.[h] But the principal acts of saving faith are accepting, receiving, and resting upon Christ alone for justification, sanctification, and eternal life, by virtue of the covenant of grace.[i]

[k]Heb 5:13-14; Rom 4:19-20; Matt 6:30; Matt 8:10.
[l]Luke 22:31-32; Eph 6:16; 1 John 5:4-5.
[m]Heb 6:11-12; Heb 10:22; Col 2:2.
[n]Heb 12:2.

3 This faith is different in degrees, weak or strong;[k] may be often and many ways assailed, and weakened, but gets the victory;[l] growing up in many to the attainment of a full assurance through Christ,[m] who is both the author and finisher of our faith.[n]

15
Of Repentance Unto Life

1 Repentance unto life is an evangelical grace,[a] the doctrine whereof is to be preached by every minister of the Gospel, as well as that of faith in Christ.[b]

[a] Zech 12:10; Acts 11:18.
[b] Luke 24:47; Mark 1:15; Acts 20:21.

2 By it, a sinner, out of the sight and sense, not only of the danger, but also of the filthiness and odiousness of his sins, as contrary to the holy nature and righteous law of God; and upon the apprehension of His mercy in Christ to such as are penitent, so grieves for, and hates his sins, as to turn from them all unto God,[c] purposing and endeavouring to walk with Him in all the ways of His commandments.[d]

[c] Ezek 18:30-31; Ezek 36:31; Isa 30:22; Ps 51:4; Jer 31:18-19; Joel 2:12-13; Amos 5:15; Ps 119:128; 2 Cor 7:11.
[d] Ps 119:6,59,106; Luke 1:6; 2 Kings 23:25.

3 Although repentance be not to be rested in, as any satisfaction for sin, or any cause of the pardon thereof,[e] which is the act of God's free grace in Christ;[f] yet is it of such necessity to all sinners, that none may expect pardon without it.[g]

[e] Ezek 36:31-32; Ezek 16:61-63.
[f] Hos 14:2,4; Rom 3:24; Eph 1:7.
[g] Luke 13:3,5; Acts 17:30-31.

4 As there is no sin so small, but it deserves damnation;[h] so there is no sin so great, that it can bring damnation upon those who truly repent.[i]

[h] Rom 6:23; Rom 5:12; Matt 12:36.
[i] Isa 55:7; Rom 8:1; Isa 1:16,18.

5 Men ought not to content themselves with a general repentance, but it is every man's duty to endeavour to repent of his particular sins, particularly.[k]

[k] Ps 19:13; Luke 19:8; 1 Tim 1:13,15.

6 As every man is bound to make private confession of his sins to God, praying for the pardon thereof;[l] upon which, and the forsaking of them, he shall find mercy;[m] so, he that scandalizeth his brother, or the Church of Christ, ought to be willing, by a private or public confession, and sorrow for his sin, to declare his repentance to those that are offended,[n] who are thereupon to be reconciled to him, and in love to receive him.[o]

[l] Ps 51:4-5,7,9,14; Ps 32:5-6.
[m] Prov 28:13; 1 John 1:9.
[n] James 5:16; Luke 17:3-4; Josh 7:19; Ps 51.
[o] 2 Cor 2:8.

16
Of Good Works

1 Good works are only such as God hath commanded in His holy Word,[a] and not such as, without the warrant thereof, are devised by men, out of blind zeal, or upon any pretence of good intention.[b]

2 These good works, done in obedience to God's commandments, are the fruits and evidences of a true and lively faith:[c] and by them believers manifest their thankfulness,[d] strengthen their assurance,[e] edify their brethren,[f] adorn the profession of the gospel,[g] stop the mouths of the adversaries,[h] and glorify God,[i] whose workmanship they are, created in Christ Jesus thereunto;[k] that, having their fruit unto holiness, they may have the end, eternal life.[l]

3 Their ability to do good works is not at all of themselves, but wholly from the Spirit of Christ.[m] And that they may be enabled thereunto, besides the graces they have already received, there is required an actual influence of the same Holy Spirit, to work in them to will, and to do, of His good pleasure:[n] yet are they not hereupon to grow negligent, as if they were not bound to perform any duty, unless upon a special motion of the Spirit; but they ought to be diligent in stirring up the grace of God that is in them.[o]

[a] Micah 6:8; Rom 12:2; Heb 13:21.
[b] Matt 15:9; Isa 29:13; 1 Pet 1:18; Rom 10:2; John 16:2; 1 Sam 15:21-23.
[c] James 2:18,22.
[d] Ps 116:12-13; 1 Pet 2:9.
[e] 1 John 2:3,5; 2 Pet 1:5-10.
[f] 2 Cor 9:2; Matt 5:16.
[g] Tit 2:5,9-12; 1 Tim 6:1.
[h] 1 Pet 2:15.
[i] 1 Pet 2:12; Phil 1:11; John 15:8.
[k] Eph 2:10.
[l] Rom 6:22.
[m] John 15:4-5; Ezek 36:26-27.
[n] Phil 2:13; Phil 4:13; 2 Cor 3:5.
[o] Phil 2:12; Heb 6:11-12; 2 Pet 1:3,5,10-11; Isa 64:7; 2 Tim 1:6; Acts 26:6-7; Jude 20-21.

4 They, who in their obedience attain to the greatest height which is possible in this life, are so far from being able to supererogate, and to do more than God requires, as that they fall short of much which in duty they are bound to do.[p]

[p] Luke 17:10; Neh 13:22; Job 9:2-3; Gal 5:17.

5 We cannot by our best works merit pardon of sin, or eternal life at the hand of God, by reason of the great disproportion that is between them and the glory to come; and the infinite distance that is between us and God, whom, by them, we can neither profit, nor satisfy for the debt of our former sins,[q] but when we have done all we can, we have done but our duty, and are unprofitable servants:[r] and because, as they are good, they proceed from His Spirit;[s] and as they are wrought by us, they are defiled, and mixed with so much weakness and imperfection, that they cannot endure the severity of God's judgment.[t]

[q] Rom 3:20; Rom 4:2,4,6; Eph 2:8-9; Tit 3:5-7; Rom 8:18; Ps 16:2; Job 22:2-3; Job 35:7-8.
[r] Luke 17:10.
[s] Gal 5:22-23.
[t] Isa 64:6; Gal 5:17; Rom 7:15,18; Ps 143:2; Ps 130:3.

6 Yet notwithstanding, the persons of believers being accepted through Christ, their good works also are accepted in Him;[u] not as though they were in this life wholly unblameable and unreprovable in God's sight;[w] but that He, looking upon them in His Son, is pleased to accept and reward that which is sincere, although accompanied with many weaknesses and imperfections.[x]

[u] Eph 1:6; 1 Pet 2:5; Exod 28:38; Gen 4:4 with Heb 11:4.
[w] Job 9:20; Ps 143:2.
[x] Heb 13:20-21; 2 Cor 8:12; Heb 6:10; Matt 25:21,23.

7 Works done by unregenerate men, although for the matter of them, they may be things which God commands, and of good use both to themselves and others:[y] yet, because they proceed not from a heart purified by faith;[z] nor are done

[y] 2 Kings 10:30-31; 1 Kings 21:27,29; Phil 1:15-16,18.
[z] Gen 4:5 with Heb 11:4; Heb 11:6.

in a right manner, according to the Word;[a] nor to a right end, the glory of God;[b] they are therefore sinful, and cannot please God, or make a man meet to receive grace from God:[c] And yet, their neglect of them is more sinful, and displeasing unto God.[d]

[a] 1 Cor 13:3; Isa 1:12.
[b] Matt 6:2,5,16.
[c] Hag 2:14; Tit 1:15; Amos 5:21-22; Hos 1:4; Rom 9:16; Tit 3:5.
[d] Ps 14:4; Ps 36:3; Job 21:14,15; Matt 25:41-43,45; Matt 23:23.

17

Of the Perseverance of the Saints

1 They, whom God hath accepted in His Beloved, effectually called, and sanctified by His Spirit, can neither totally nor finally fall away from the state of grace: but shall certainly persevere therein to the end, and be eternally saved.[a]

2 This perseverance of the saints depends not upon their own free will, but upon the immutability of the decree of election, flowing from the free and unchangeable love of God the Father;[b] upon the efficacy of the merit and intercession of Jesus Christ,[c] the abiding of the Spirit, and of the seed of God within them,[d] and the nature of the covenant of grace:[e] from all which ariseth also the certainty and infallibility thereof.[f]

3 Nevertheless, they may, through the temptations of Satan and of the world, the prevalency of corruption remaining in them, and the neglect of the means of their preservation, fall into grievous sins;[g] and, for a time, continue therein:[h] whereby they incur God's displeasure,[i] and grieve His Holy Spirit,[k] come to be deprived of some measure of their graces and comforts,[l] have their hearts hardened,[m] and their consciences wounded;[n] hurt and scandalize others,[o] and bring temporal judgments upon themselves.[p]

[a]Phil 1:6; 2 Pet 1:10; John 10:28-29; 1 John 3:9; 1 Pet 1:5,9. [b]2 Tim 2:18-19; Jer 31:3. [c]Heb 10:10,14; Heb 13:20-21; Heb 9:12-15; Rom 8:33-39; John 17:11,24; Luke 22:32; Heb 7:25. [d]John 14:16-17; 1 John 2:27; 1 John 3:9. [e]Jer 32:40. [f]John 10:28; 2 Thess 3:3; 1 John 2:19. [g]Matt 26:70,72,74. [h]Ps 51. [i]Isa 64:5,7,9; 2 Sam 11:27. [k]Eph 4:30. [l]Ps 51:8,10,12; Rev 2:4; Song 5:2-4,6. [m]Isa 63:17; Mark 6:52; Mark 16:14. [n]Ps 32:3-4; Ps 51:8. [o]2 Sam 12:14. [p]Ps 89:31-32; 1 Cor 11:32.

18
Of Assurance of Grace and Salvation

1 Although hypocrites and other unregenerate men may vainly deceive themselves with false hopes and carnal presumptions of being in the favour of God, and estate of salvation[a] which hope of theirs shall perish:[b] yet such as truly believe in the Lord Jesus, and love Him in sincerity, endeavouring to walk in all good conscience before Him, may, in this life, be certainly assured that they are in the state of grace,[c] and may rejoice in the hope of the glory of God, which hope shall never make them ashamed.[d]

[a] Job 8:13-14; Micah 3:11; Deut 29:19; John 8:41.
[b] Matt 7:22-23.
[c] 1 John 2:3; 1 John 3:14,18-19, 21,24; 1 John 5:13.
[d] Rom 5:2,5.

2 This certainty is not a bare conjectural and probable persuasion, grounded upon a fallible hope;[e] but an infallible assurance of faith, founded upon the divine truth of the promises of salvation,[f] the inward evidence of those graces unto which these promises are made,[g] the testimony of the Spirit of adoption witnessing with our spirits that we are the children of God,[h] which Spirit is the earnest of our inheritance, whereby we are sealed to the day of redemption.[i]

[e] Heb 6:11,19.
[f] Heb 6:17-18.
[g] 2 Pet 1:4,5,10-11; 1 John 2:3; 1 John 3:14; 2 Cor 1:12.
[h] Rom 8:15-16.
[i] Eph 1:13-14; Eph 4:30; 2 Cor 1:21-22.

3 This infallible assurance doth not so belong to the essence of faith, but that a true believer may wait long, and conflict with many difficulties before he be partaker of it:[k] yet, being enabled by the Spirit to know the things which are freely given him of God, he may without extraordinary revelation, in the right use of ordinary means,

[k] 1 John 5:13; Isa 50:10; Mark 9:24; Ps 88; Ps 77:1-12.

attain thereunto.[l] And therefore it is the duty of everyone to give all diligence to make his calling and election sure,[m] that thereby his heart may be enlarged in peace and joy in the Holy Ghost, in love and thankfulness to God, and in strength and cheerfulness in the duties of obedience, the proper fruits of this assurance;[n] so far is it from inclining men to looseness.[o]

4 True believers may have the assurance of their salvation divers ways shaken, diminished, and intermitted; as, by negligence in preserving of it, by falling into some special sin, which woundeth the conscience and grieveth the Spirit; by some sudden or vehement temptation, by God's withdrawing the light of His countenance, and suffering even such as fear Him to walk in darkness and to have no light:[p] yet are they never utterly destitute of that seed of God, and life of faith, that love of Christ and the brethren, that sincerity of heart, and conscience of duty, out of which, by the operation of the Spirit, this assurance may, in due time, be revived;[q] and by the which, in the mean time, they are supported from utter despair.[r]

[l] 1 Cor 2:12; 1 John 4:13; Heb 6:11-12; Eph 3:17-19.
[m] 2 Pet 1:10.
[n] Rom 5:1-2,5; Rom 14:17; Rom 15:13; Eph 1:3-4; Ps 4:6-7; Ps 119:32.
[o] 1 John 2:1-2; Rom 6:1-2; Tit 2:11-12,14; 2 Cor 7:1; Rom 8:1,12; 1 John 3:2-3; Ps 130:4; 1 John 1:6-7.
[p] Song 5:2-3,6; Ps 51:8,12,14; Eph 4:30-31; Ps 77:1-10; Matt 26:69-72; Ps 31:22; Ps 88; Isa 50:10.
[q] 1 John 3:9; Luke 22:32; Job 13:15; Ps 73:15; Ps 51:8,12; Isa 50:10.
[r] Micah 7:7-9; Jer 32:40; Isa 54:7-10; Ps 22:1; Ps 88.

19
Of the Law of God

1 God gave to Adam a law, as a covenant of works, by which He bound him and all his posterity to personal, entire, exact, and perpetual obedience; promised life upon the fulfilling, and threatened death upon the breach of it; and endued him with power and ability to keep it.[a]

[a] Gen 1:26-27 with Gen 2:17; Rom 2:14-15; Rom 10:5; Rom 5:12,19; Gal 3:10,12; Eccl 7:29; Job 28:28.

2 This law, after his fall, continued to be a perfect rule of righteousness; and, as such, was delivered by God upon Mount Sinai, in ten commandments, and written in two tables:[b] the four first commandments containing our duty towards God; and the other six, our duty to man.[c]

[b] James 1:25; James 2:8,10-12; Rom 13:8-9; Deut 5:32; Deut 10:4; Exod 34:1.
[c] Matt 22:37-40.

3 Beside this law, commonly called moral, God was pleased to give to the people of Israel, as a church under age, ceremonial laws, containing several typical ordinances, partly of worship, prefiguring Christ, His graces, actions, sufferings, and benefits;[d] and partly holding forth divers instructions of moral duties.[e] All which ceremonial laws are now abrogated, under the New Testament.[f]

[d] Heb chap 9; Heb 10:1; Gal 4:1-3; Col 2:17.
[e] 1 Cor 5:7; 2 Cor 6:17; Jude 23.
[f] Col 2:14-17; Dan 9:27; Eph 2:15-16.

4 To them also, as a body politic, He gave sundry judicial laws, which expired together with the State of that people; not obliging any other now, further than the general equity thereof may require.[g]

[g] Exod chap 21; Exod 22:1-29; Gen 49:10 with 1 Pet 2:13-14; Matt 5:17 with Matt 5:38-39; 1 Cor 9:8-10.

5 The moral law doth for ever bind all, as well justified persons as others, to the obedience thereof;[h] and that, not only in regard of the matter contained in it, but also in respect of the authority of God the Creator, who gave it.[i] Neither doth Christ, in the gospel, any way dissolve, but much strengthen this obligation.[k]

6 Although true believers be not under the law, as a covenant of works, to be thereby justified or condemned;[l] yet is it of great use to them, as well as to others; in that, as a rule of life informing them of the will of God, and their duty, it directs and binds them to walk accordingly;[m] discovering also the sinful pollutions of their nature, hearts and lives;[n] so as, examining themselves thereby, they may come to further conviction of, humiliation for, and hatred against sin;[o] together with a clearer sight of the need they have of Christ, and the perfection of His obedience.[p] It is likewise of use to the regenerate, to restrain their corruptions, in that it forbids sin:[q] and the threatenings of it serve to show what even their sins deserve; and what afflictions, in this life, they may expect for them, although freed from the curse thereof threatened in the law.[r] The promises of it, in like manner, show them God's approbation of obedience, and what blessings they may expect upon the performance thereof:[s] although not as due to them by the law as a covenant of works.[t] So as, a man's doing good, and refraining from evil, because the law encourageth to the one, and deterreth from the

[h] Rom 13:8-10; Eph 6:2; 1 John 2:3-4,7-8.
[i] James 2:10-11.
[k] Matt 5:17-19; James 2:8; Rom 3:31.
[l] Rom 6:14; Gal 2:16; Gal 3:13; Gal 4:4-5; Acts 13:39; Rom 8:1.
[m] Rom 7:12-22,25; Ps 119:4-6; 1 Cor 7:19; Gal 5:14,16,18-23.
[n] Rom 7:7; Rom 3:20.
[o] James 1:23-25; Rom 7:9,14,24.
[p] Gal 3:24; Rom 7:24-25; Rom 8:3-4.
[q] James 2:11; Ps 119:101,104,128.
[r] Ezra 9:13-14; Ps 89:30-34.
[s] Lev 26:1-14 with 2 Cor 6:16; Eph 6:2-3; Ps 37:11 with Matt 5:5; Ps 19:11.
[t] Gal 2:16; Luke 17:10.

other, is no evidence of his being under the law; and, not under grace.[u]

[u]Rom 6:12,14; 1 Pet 3:8-12 with Ps 34:12-16; Heb 12:28-29.

7 Neither are the forementioned uses of the law contrary to the grace of the Gospel, but do sweetly comply with it;[w] the Spirit of Christ subduing and enabling the will of man to do that freely, and cheerfully, which the will of God, revealed in the law, requireth to be done.[x]

[w]Gal 3:21.

[x]Ezek 36:27; Heb 8:10 with Jer 31:33.

20

Of Christian Liberty, and Liberty of Conscience

1 The liberty which Christ hath purchased for believers under the gospel consists in their freedom from the guilt of sin, the condemning wrath of God, the curse of the moral law;[a] and, in their being delivered from this present evil world, bondage to Satan, and dominion of sin;[b] from the evil of afflictions, the sting of death, the victory of the grave, and everlasting damnation;[c] as also, in their free access to God,[d] and their yielding obedience unto Him, not out of slavish fear, but a childlike love and willing mind.[e] All which were common also to believers under the law.[f] But, under the New Testament, the liberty of Christians is further enlarged, in their freedom from the yoke of the ceremonial law, to which the Jewish Church was subjected;[g] and in greater boldness of access to the throne of grace,[h] and in fuller communications of the free Spirit of God, than believers under the law did ordinarily partake of.[i]

2 God alone is Lord of the conscience,[k] and hath left it free from the doctrines and commandments of men, which are in any thing contrary to His Word; or beside it, if matters of faith or worship.[l] So that, to believe such doctrines, or to obey such commands, out of conscience, is to betray true liberty of conscience:[m] and the requiring of an implicit faith, and an absolute and blind obedience is to destroy liberty of conscience, and reason also.[n]

[a] *Tit 2:14; 1 Thess 1:10; Gal 3:13.*
[b] *Gal 1:4; Col 1:13; Acts 26:18; Rom 6:14.*
[c] *Rom 8:28; Ps 119:71; 1 Cor 15:54-57; Rom 8:1.*
[d] *Rom 5:1-2.*
[e] *Rom 8:14-15; 1 John 4:18.*
[f] *Gal 3:9,14.*
[g] *Gal 4:1-3,6-7; Gal 5:1; Acts 15:10-11.*
[h] *Heb 4:14,16; Heb 10:19-22.*
[i] *John 7:38-39; 2 Cor 3:13,17-18.*
[k] *James 4:12; Rom 14:4.*
[l] *Acts 4:19; Acts 5:29; 1 Cor 7:23; Matt 23:8-10; 2 Cor 1:24; Matt 15:9.*
[m] *Col 2:20,22-23; Gal 1:10; Gal 2:4-5; Gal 5:1.*
[n] *Rom 10:17; Rom 14:23; Isa 8:20; Acts 17:11; John 4:22; Hos 5:11;*

3 They who, upon pretence of Christian liberty, do practise any sin, or cherish any lust, do thereby destroy the end of Christian liberty, which is, that being delivered out of the hands of our enemies, we might serve the Lord, without fear, in holiness and righteousness before Him, all the days of our life.[o]

4 And because the powers which God hath ordained, and the liberty which Christ hath purchased, are not intended by God to destroy, but mutually to uphold and preserve one another, they who, upon pretence of Christian liberty, shall oppose any lawful power, or the lawful exercise of it, whether it be civil or ecclesiastical, resist the ordinance of God.[p] And, for their publishing of such opinions, or maintaining of such practices, as are contrary to the light of nature, or to the known principles of Christianity whether concerning faith, worship, or conversation, or to the power of godliness; or, such erroneous opinions or practices, as either in their own nature, or in the manner of publishing or maintaining them, are destructive to the external peace and order which Christ hath established in the Church, they may lawfully be called to account, and proceeded against by the censures of the Church,[q] and by the power of the civil magistrate.[r]

Rev 13:12,16-17; Jer 8:9.

[o]Gal 5:13; 1 Pet 2:16; 2 Pet 2:19; John 8:34; Luke 1:74-75.

[p]Matt 12:25; 1 Pet 2:13-14,16; Rom 13:1-8; Heb 13:17.

[q]Rom 1:32 with 1 Cor 5:1,5,11,13; 2 John 10-11 and 2 Thess 3:14 and 1 Tim 6:3-5 and Tit 1:10-11,13 and Tit 3:10 with Matt 18:15-17; 1 Tim 1:19-20; Rev 2:2,14-15,20; Rev 3:9.

[r]Deut 13:6-12; Rom 13:3-4 with 2 John 10-11; Ezra 7:23,25-28; Rev 17:12,16-17; Neh 13:15,17, 21-22,25,30; 2 Kings 23:5-6,9, 20-21; 2 Chron 34:33; 2 Chron 15:12-13,16; Dan 3:29; 1 Tim 2:2; Isa 49:23; Zech 13:2-3.

21

Of Religious Worship, and the Sabbath Day

1 The light of nature showeth that there is a God, who hath lordship and sovereignty over all, is good, and doth good unto all, and is therefore to be feared, loved, praised, called upon, trusted in, and served, with all the heart, and with all the soul, and with all the might.[a] But the acceptable way of worshipping the true God is instituted by Himself, and so limited by His own revealed will, that He may not be worshipped according to the imaginations and devices of men, or the suggestions of Satan, under any visible representation, or any other way not prescribed in the Holy Scripture.[b]

2 Religious worship is to be given to God, the Father, Son, and Holy Ghost; and to Him alone;[c] not to angels, saints, or any other creature:[d] and since the fall, not without a Mediator; nor in the mediation of any other but of Christ alone.[e]

3 Prayer, with thanksgiving, being one special part of religious worship,[f] is by God required of all men:[g] and that it may be accepted, it is to be made in the name of the Son,[h] by the help of His Spirit,[i] according to His will,[k] with understanding, reverence, humility, fervency, faith, love, and perseverance;[l] and, if vocal, in a known tongue.[m]

4 Prayer is to be made for things lawful;[n] and for all sorts of men living, or that shall live hereafter:[o] but not for the dead,[p] nor for those of

[a] Rom 1:20; Acts 17:24; Ps 119:68; Jer 10:7; Ps 31:23; Ps 18:3; Rom 10:12; Ps 62:8; Josh 24:14; Mark 12:33.
[b] Deut 12:32; Matt 15:9; Acts 17:25; Matt 4:9-10; Deut 4:15-20; Exod 20:4-6; Col 2:23.
[c] Matt 4:10 with John 5:23 and 2 Cor 13:14.
[d] Col 2:18; Rev 19:10; Rom 1:25.
[e] John 14:6; 1 Tim 2:5; Eph 2:18; Col 3:17.
[f] Phil 4:6. [g] Ps 65:2.
[h] John 14:13-14; 1 Pet 2:5.
[i] Rom 8:26.
[k] 1 John 5:14.
[l] Ps 47:7; Eccl 5:1-2; Heb 12:28; Gen 18:27; James 1:6-7; 5:16; Mark 11:24; Matt 6:12,14-15; Col 4:2; Eph 6:18.
[m] 1 Cor 14:14.
[n] 1 John 5:14.

whom it may be known that they have sinned the sin unto death.[q]

5 The reading of the Scriptures with godly fear,[r] the sound preaching[s] and conscionable hearing of the Word, in obedience unto God, with understanding, faith, and reverence;[t] singing of psalms with grace in the heart;[u] as also, the due administration and worthy receiving of the sacraments instituted by Christ; are all parts of the ordinary religious worship of God:[w] beside religious oaths,[x] vows,[y] solemn fastings,[z] and thanksgivings, upon special occasions,[a] which are, in their several times and seasons, to be used in a holy and religious manner.[b]

6 Neither prayer, nor any other part of religious worship, is now, under the Gospel, either tied unto, or made more acceptable by any place in which it is performed, or towards which it is directed:[c] but God is to be worshipped everywhere,[d] in spirit and truth;[e] as in private families[f] daily,[g] and in secret each one by himself;[h] so, more solemnly, in the public assemblies, which are not carelessly or wilfully to be neglected, or forsaken, when God, by His Word or providence, calleth thereunto.[i]

7 As it is the law of nature, that, in general, a due proportion of time be set apart for the worship of God; so, in His Word, by a positive, moral, and perpetual commandment, binding all men in all ages, He hath particularly appointed one day in seven, for a Sabbath, to be kept holy

[o] *1 Tim 2:1-2; John 17:20; 2 Sam 7:29; Ruth 4:12.*
[p] *2 Sam 12:21-23 with Luke 16:25-26; Rev 14:13.*
[q] *1 John 5:16.*
[r] *Acts 15:21; Rev 1:3.*
[s] *2 Tim 4:2.*
[t] *James 1:22; Acts 10:33; Matt 13:19; Heb 4:2; Isa 66:2.*
[u] *Col 3:16; Eph 5:19; James 5:13.*
[w] *Matt 28:19; 1 Cor 11:23-29; Acts 2:42.*
[x] *Deut 6:13 with Neh 10:29.*
[y] *Isa 19:21 with Eccl 5:4-5.*
[z] *Joel 2:12; Esth 4:16; Matt 9:15; 1 Cor 7:5.*
[a] *Ps 107; Esth 9:22.*
[b] *Heb 12:28.*
[c] *John 4:21.*
[d] *Mal 1:11; 1 Tim 2:8.*
[e] *John 4:23-24.*
[f] *Jer 10:25; Deut 6:6-7; Job 1:5; 2 Sam 6:18,20; 1 Pet 3:7; Acts 10:2.*
[g] *Matt 6:11.*
[h] *Matt 6:6; Eph 6:18.*
[i] *Isa 56:6,7; Heb 10:25; Prov 1:20,21,24; Prov 8:34; Acts 13:42; Luke 4:16; Acts 2:42.*

unto Him:[k] which, from the beginning of the world to the resurrection of Christ, was the last day of the week; and, from the resurrection of Christ, was changed into the first day of the week,[l] which, in Scripture, is called the Lord's Day,[m] and is to be continued to the end of the world, as the Christian Sabbath.[n]

[k] *Exod 20:8,10-11; Isa 56:2,4,6-7.*
[l] *Gen 2:2-3; 1 Cor 16:1-2; Acts 20:7.*
[m] *Rev 1:10.*
[n] *Exod 20:8,10 with Matt 5:17-18.*

8 This Sabbath is then kept holy unto the Lord, when men, after a due preparing of their hearts, and ordering of their common affairs beforehand, do not only observe an holy rest, all the day, from their own works, words, and thoughts about their worldly employments, and recreations,[o] but also are taken up, the whole time, in the public and private exercises of His worship, and in the duties of necessity and mercy.[p]

[o] *Exod 20:8; Exod 16:23,25-26, 29-30; Exod 31:15-17; Isa 58:13; Neh 13:15-19,21-22.*
[p] *Isa 58:13; Matt 12:1-13.*

22
Of Lawful Oaths and Vows

1 A lawful oath is a part of religious worship,[a] wherein, upon just occasion, the person swearing solemnly calleth God to witness what he asserteth, or promiseth; and to judge him according to the truth or falsehood of what he sweareth.[b]

[a]Deut 10:20.
[b]Exod 20:7; Lev 19:12; 2 Cor 1:23; 2 Chron 6:22-23.

2 The name of God only is that by which men ought to swear, and therein it is to be used with all holy fear and reverence.[c] Therefore, to swear vainly or rashly, by that glorious and dreadful Name; or, to swear at all by any other thing, is sinful, and to be abhorred.[d] Yet, as in matters of weight and moment, an oath is warranted by the Word of God, under the New Testament, as well as under the Old;[e] so a lawful oath, being imposed by lawful authority, in such matters ought to be taken.[f]

[c]Deut 6:13.
[d]Exod 20:7; Jer 5:7; Matt 5:34,37; James 5:12.
[e]Heb 6:16; 2 Cor 1:23; Isa 65:16.
[f]1 Kings 8:31; Neh 13:25; Ezra 10:5.

3 Whosoever taketh an oath ought duly to consider the weightiness of so solemn an act, and therein to avouch nothing but what he is fully persuaded is the truth:[g] neither may any man bind himself by oath to anything but what is good and just, and what he believeth so to be, and what he is able and resolved to perform.[h] Yet is it a sin to refuse an oath touching anything that is good and just, being imposed by lawful authority.[i]

[g]Exod 20:7; Jer 4:2.
[h]Gen 24:2-3, 5-6,8-9.
[i]Num 5:19,21; Neh 5:12; Exod 22:7-11.

4 An oath is to be taken in the plain and common sense of the words, without equivocation, or

[k] Jer 4:2; Ps 24:4.
[l] 1 Sam 25:22,32-34; Ps 15:4.
[m] Ezek 17:16,18-19; Josh 9:18-19 with 2 Sam 21:1.

mental reservation.[k] It cannot oblige to sin; but in anything not sinful, being taken, it binds to performance, although to a man's own hurt.[l] Nor is it to be violated, although made to heretics, or infidels.[m]

5 A vow is of the like nature with a promissory oath, and ought to be made with the like religious care, and to be performed with the like faithfulness.[n]

[n] Isa 19:21; Eccl 5:4-6; Ps 61:8; Ps 66:13-14.

6 It is not to be made to any creature, but to God alone:[o] and, that it may be accepted, it is to be made voluntarily, out of faith, and conscience of duty, in way of thankfulness for mercy received, or for the obtaining of what we want, whereby we more strictly bind ourselves to necessary duties; or, to other things, so far and so long as they may fitly conduce thereunto.[p]

[o] Ps 76:11; Jer 44:25-26.
[p] Deut 23:21-23; Ps 50:14; Gen 28:20-22; 1 Sam 1:11; Ps 66:13-14; Ps 132:2-5.

7 No man may vow to do anything forbidden in the Word of God, or what would hinder any duty therein commanded, or which is not in his own power, and for the performance whereof he hath no promise of ability from God.[q] In which respects, Popish monastical vows of perpetual single life, professed poverty, and regular obedience, are so far from being degrees of higher perfection, that they are superstitious and sinful snares, in which no Christian may entangle himself.[r]

[q] Acts 23:12,14; Mark 6:26; Num 30:5,8,12-13.
[r] Matt 19:11-12; 1 Cor 7:2,9; Eph 4:28; 1 Pet 4:2; 1 Cor 7:23.

23
Of the Civil Magistrate

1 God, the supreme Lord and King of all the world, hath ordained civil magistrates, to be, under Him, over the people, for His own glory, and the public good: and, to this end, hath armed them with the power of the sword, for the defence and encouragement of them that are good, and for the punishment of evildoers.[a]

[a] *Rom 13:1-4; 1 Pet 2:13-14.*

2 It is lawful for Christians to accept and execute the office of a magistrate, when called thereunto:[b] in the managing whereof, as they ought especially to maintain piety, justice, and peace, according to the wholesome laws of each commonwealth;[c] so for that end, they may lawfully now, under the New Testament, wage war, upon just and necessary occasion.[d]

[b] *Prov 8:15-16; Rom 13:1-2,4.*
[c] *Ps 2:10-12; 1 Tim 2:2; Ps 82:3-4; 2 Sam 23:3; 1 Pet 2:13.*
[d] *Luke 3:14; Rom 13:4; Matt 8:9-10; Acts 10:1-2; Rev 17:14,16.*

3 The civil magistrate may not assume to himself the administration of the Word and sacraments; or the power of the keys of the kingdom of heaven;[e] yet he hath authority, and it is his duty, to take order, that unity and peace be preserved in the Church, that the truth of God be kept pure and entire; that all blasphemies and heresies be suppressed; all corruptions and abuses in worship and discipline prevented or reformed; and all the ordinances of God duly settled, administered, and observed.[f] For the better effecting whereof, he hath power to call synods, to be present at them, and

[e] *2 Chron 26:18 with Matt 18:17 and Matt 16:19; 1 Cor 12:28-29; Eph 4:11-12; 1 Cor 4:1-2; Rom 10:15; Heb 5:4.*
[f] *Isa 49:23; Ps 122:9; Ezra 7:23,25-28; Lev 24:16; Deut 13:5-6,12; 2 Kings 18:4; 1 Chron 13:1-9; 2 Kings 23:1-26; 2 Chron 34:33; 2 Chron 15:12-13.*

to provide that whatsoever is transacted in them be according to the mind of God.[g]

[g] 2 Chron 19:8-11; 2 Chron chap 29-30; Matt 2:4-5.

4 It is the duty of people to pray for magistrates,[h] to honour their persons,[i] to pay them tribute and other dues,[k] to obey their lawful commands, and to be subject to their authority, for conscience' sake.[l] Infidelity, or difference in religion, doth not make void the magistrates' just and legal authority, nor free the people from their due obedience to them:[m] from which ecclesiastical persons are not exempted,[n] much less hath the Pope any power and jurisdiction over them in their dominions, or over any of their people; and, least of all, to deprive them of their dominions, or lives, if he shall judge them to be heretics, or upon any other pretence whatsoever.[o]

[h] 1 Tim 2:1-2.

[i] 1 Pet 2:17.

[k] Rom 13:6-7.

[l] Rom 13:5; Tit 3:1.

[m] 1 Pet 2:13-14,16.

[n] Rom 13:1; 1 Kings 2:35; Acts 25:9-11; 2 Pet 2:1,10-11; Jude 8-11.

[o] 2 Thess 2:4; Rev 13:15-17.

24
Of Marriage and Divorce

1 Marriage is to be between one man and one woman: neither is it lawful for any man to have more than one wife, nor for any woman to have more than one husband, at the same time.[a]

[a]Gen 2:24; Matt 19:5-6; Prov 2:17.

2 Marriage was ordained for the mutual help of husband and wife,[b] for the increase of mankind with a legitimate issue, and of the Church with an holy seed;[c] and for preventing of uncleanness.[d]

[b]Gen 2:18.
[c]Mal 2:15.
[d]1 Cor 7:2,9.

3 It is lawful for all sorts of people to marry, who are able with judgment to give their consent.[e] Yet it is the duty of Christians to marry only in the Lord.[f] And therefore such as profess the true reformed religion should not marry with infidels, papists, or other idolaters: neither should such as are godly be unequally yoked, by marrying with such as are notoriously wicked in their life, or maintain damnable heresies.[g]

[e]Heb 13:4; 1 Tim 4:3; 1 Cor 7:36-38; Gen 24:57-58.
[f]1 Cor 7:39.
[g]Gen 34:14; Exod 34:16; Deut 7:3-4; 1 Kings 11:4; Neh 13:25-27; Mal 2:11-12; 2 Cor 6:14.

4 Marriage ought not to be within the degrees of consanguinity or affinity forbidden in the Word.[h] Nor can such incestuous marriages ever be made lawful by any law of man or consent of parties, so as those persons may live together as man and wife.[i] The man may not marry any of his wife's kindred nearer in blood than he may of his own; nor the woman of her husband's kindred nearer in blood than of her own.[k]

[h]Lev chap 18; 1 Cor 5:1; Amos 2:7.
[i]Mark 6:18; Lev 18:24-28.
[k]Lev 20:19-21.

5 Adultery or fornication committed after a contract, being detected before marriage, giveth just occasion to the innocent party to dissolve that contract.[l] In the case of adultery after marriage, it is lawful for the innocent party to sue out a divorce:[m] and, after the divorce, to marry another, as if the offending party were dead.[n]

[l] *Matt 1:18-20.*
[m] *Matt 5:31-32.*
[n] *Matt 19:9; Rom 7:2-3.*

6 Although the corruption of man be such as is apt to study arguments unduly to put asunder those whom God hath joined together in marriage: yet nothing but adultery, or such wilful desertion as can no way be remedied by the Church or civil magistrate, is cause sufficient of dissolving the bond of marriage:[o] wherein, a public and orderly course of proceeding is to be observed; and the persons concerned in it not left to their own wills and discretion, in their own case.[p]

[o] *Matt 19:8-9; 1 Cor 7:15; Matt 19:6.*
[p] *Deut 24:1-4.*

25
Of the Church

1 The catholic or universal Church, which is invisible, consists of the whole number of the elect, that have been, are, or shall be gathered into one, under Christ the Head thereof; and is the spouse, the body, the fulness of Him that filleth all in all.[a]

2 The visible Church, which is also catholic or universal under the Gospel (not confined to one nation as before under the law), consists of all those throughout the world that profess the true religion;[b] and of their children:[c] and is the kingdom of the Lord Jesus Christ,[d] the house and family of God,[e] out of which there is no ordinary possibility of salvation.[f]

3 Unto this catholic visible Church, Christ hath given the ministry, oracles, and ordinances of God, for the gathering and perfecting of the saints, in this life, to the end of the world: and doth, by His own presence and Spirit, according to His promise, make them effectual thereunto.[g]

4 This catholic Church hath been sometimes more, sometimes less visible.[h] And particular Churches, which are members thereof, are more or less pure, according as the doctrine of the Gospel is taught and embraced, ordinances administered, and public worship performed more or less purely in them.[i]

[a] *Eph 1:10,22-23; Eph 5:23,27,32; Col 1:18.*
[b] *1 Cor 1:2; 1 Cor 12:12-13; Ps 2:8; Rev 7:9; Rom 15:9-12.*
[c] *1 Cor 7:14; Acts 2:39; Ezek 16:20,21; Rom 11:16; Gen 3:15; Gen 17:7.*
[d] *Matt 13:47; Isa 9:7.*
[e] *Eph 2:19; Eph 3:15.*
[f] *Acts 2:47.*
[g] *1 Cor 12:28; Eph 4:11-13; Matt 28:19,20; Isa 59:21.*
[h] *Rom 11:3-4; Rev 12:6,14.*
[i] *Rev chap 2-3; 1 Cor 5:6-7.*

5 The purest Churches under heaven are subject both to mixture and error;[k] and some have so degenerated, as to become no Churches of Christ, but synagogues of Satan.[l] Nevertheless, there shall be always a Church on earth, to worship God according to His will.[m]

[k] *1 Cor 13:12; Rev chap 2-3; Matt 13:24-30,47.*
[l] *Rev 18:2; Rom 11:18-22.*
[m] *Matt 16:18; Ps 72:17; Ps 102:28; Matt 28:19-20.*

6 There is no other head of the Church but the Lord Jesus Christ.[n] Nor can the Pope of Rome, in any sense, be head thereof. But is that Antichrist, that man of sin, and son of perdition, that exalteth himself, in the Church, against Christ and all that is called God.[o]

[n] *Col 1:18; Eph 1:22.*
[o] *Matt 23:8-10; 2 Thess 2:3-4,8-9; Rev 13:6.*

26
Of the Communion of Saints

1 All saints, that are united to Jesus Christ their Head, by His Spirit, and by faith, have fellowship with Him in His graces, sufferings, death, resurrection, and glory:[a] and, being united to one another in love, they have communion in each other's gifts and graces,[b] and are obliged to the performance of such duties, public and private, as do conduce to their mutual good, both in the inward and outward man.[c]

[a] *1 John 1:3; Eph 3:16-19; John 1:16; Eph 2:5-6; Phil 3:10; Rom 6:5-6; 2 Tim 2:12.*
[b] *Eph 4:15-16; 1 Cor 12:7; 1 Cor 3:21-23; Col 2:19.*
[c] *1 Thess 5:11,14; Rom 1:11-12,14; 1 John 3:16-18; Gal 6:10.*

2 Saints by profession are bound to maintain a holy fellowship and communion in the worship of God, and in performing such other spiritual services as tend to their mutual edification;[d] as also in relieving each other in outward things, according to their several abilities, and necessities. Which communion, as God offereth opportunity, is to be extended unto all those who, in every place, call upon the name of the Lord Jesus.[e]

[d] *Heb 10:24-25; Acts 2:42,46; Isa 2:3; 1 Cor 11:20.*
[e] *Acts 2:44-45; 1 John 3:17; 2 Cor chap 8-9; Acts 11:29-30.*

3 This communion which the saints have with Christ, doth not make them in any wise, partakers of the substance of His Godhead; or to be equal with Christ in any respect: either of which to affirm is impious and blasphemous.[f] Nor doth their communion one with another, as saints, take away, or infringe the title or property which each man hath in his goods and possessions.[g]

[f] *Col 1:18-19; 1 Cor 8:6; Isa 42:8; 1 Tim 6:15-16; Ps 45:7 with Heb 1:8-9.*
[g] *Exod 20:15; Eph 4:28; Acts 5:4.*

27
Of the Sacraments

[a]Rom 4:11; Gen 17:7,10. [b]Matt 28:19; 1 Cor 11:23. [c]1 Cor 10:16; 1 Cor 11:25-26; Gal 3:17. [d]Rom 15:8; Exod 12:48; Gen 34:14. [e]Rom 6:3-4; 1 Cor 10:16,21.

1 Sacraments are holy signs and seals of the covenant of grace,[a] immediately instituted by God, to represent Christ and His benefits; and to confirm our interest in Him:[c] as also, to put a visible difference between those that belong unto the Church, and the rest of the world;[d] and solemnly to engage them to the service of God in Christ, according to His Word.[e]

[f]Gen 17:10; Matt 26:27-28; Tit 3:5.

2 There is, in every sacrament, a spiritual relation, or sacramental union, between the sign and the thing signified: whence it comes to pass, that the names and effects of the one are attributed to the other.[f]

[g]Rom 2:28-29; 1 Pet 3:21. [h]Matt 3:11; 1 Cor 12:13. [i]Matt 26:27-28; Matt 28:19-20.

3 The grace which is exhibited in or by the sacraments rightly used, is not conferred by any power in them; neither doth the efficacy of a sacrament depend upon the piety or intention of him that doth administer it:[g] but upon the work of the Spirit,[h] and the word of institution, which contains, together with a precept authorizing the use thereof, a promise of benefit to worthy receivers.[i]

[k]Matt 28:19; 1 Cor 11:20,23; 1 Cor 4:1; Heb 5:4.

4 There be only two sacraments ordained by Christ our Lord in the Gospel; that is to say, Baptism and the Supper of the Lord: neither of which may be dispensed by any but by a minister of the Word lawfully ordained.[k]

5 The sacraments of the Old Testament, in regard of the spiritual things thereby signified and exhibited, were, for substance, the same with those of the New.[l]

[l] 1 Cor 10:1-4.

28
Of Baptism

1 Baptism is a sacrament of the New Testament, ordained by Jesus Christ,[a] not only for the solemn admission of the party baptized into the visible Church;[b] but also, to be unto him a sign and seal of the covenant of grace,[c] of his ingrafting into Christ,[d] of regeneration,[e] of remission of sins,[f] and of his giving up unto God through Jesus Christ, to walk in newness of life.[g] Which sacrament is, by Christ's own appointment, to be continued in His Church until the end of the world.[h]

2 The outward element to be used in this sacrament is water, wherewith the party is to be baptized, in the name of the Father, and of the Son, and of the Holy Ghost, by a minister of the Gospel, lawfully called thereunto.[i]

3 Dipping of the person into the water is not necessary: but Baptism is rightly administered by pouring or sprinkling water upon the person.[k]

4 Not only those that do actually profess faith in and obedience unto Christ,[l] but also the infants of one or both believing parents, are to be baptized.[m]

5 Although it be a great sin to contemn or neglect this ordinance,[n] yet grace and salvation are not so inseparably annexed unto it, as that no person

[a] *Matt 28:19.*
[b] *1 Cor 12:13.*
[c] *Rom 4:11 with Col 2:11-12.*
[d] *Gal 3:27; Rom 6:5.*
[e] *Tit 3:5.*
[f] *Mark 1:4.*
[g] *Rom 6:3-4.*
[h] *Matt 28:19-20.*
[i] *Matt 3:11; John 1:33; Matt 28:19-20.*
[k] *Heb 9:10,19-22; Acts 2:41; Acts 16:33; Mark 7:4.*
[l] *Mark 16:15-16; Acts 8:37-38.*
[m] *Gen 17:7,9-10 with Gal 3:9,14 and Col 2:11-12 and Acts 2:38-39 and Rom 4:11-12; 1 Cor 7:14; Matt 28:19; Mark 10:13-16; Luke 18:15.*
[n] *Luke 7:30 with Exod 4:24-26.*

can be regenerated or saved without it;[o] or, that all that are baptized are undoubtedly regenerated.[p]

[o]Rom 4:11; Acts 10:2,4,22,31, 45,47.

[p]Acts 8:13,23.

6 The efficacy of Baptism is not tied to that moment of time wherein it is administered;[q] yet notwithstanding, by the right use of this ordinance, the grace promised is not only offered, but really exhibited and conferred, by the Holy Ghost, to such (whether of age or infants) as that grace belongeth unto, according to the counsel of God's own will, in His appointed time.[r]

[q]John 3:5,8.

[r]Gal 3:27; Tit 3:5; Eph 5:25-26; Acts 2:38,41.

7 The sacrament of Baptism is but once to be administered unto any person.[s]

[s]Tit 3:5.

29

Of the Lord's Supper

1 Our Lord Jesus, in the night wherein He was betrayed, instituted the sacrament of His body and blood, called the Lord's Supper, to be observed in His Church, unto the end of the world, for the perpetual remembrance of the sacrifice of Himself in His death; the sealing all benefits thereof unto true believers, their spiritual nourishment and growth in Him, their further engagement in and to all duties which they owe unto Him; and to be a bond and pledge of their communion with Him, and with each other, as members of His mystical body.[a]

[a] *1 Cor 11:23-26; 1 Cor 10:16-17,21; 1 Cor 12:13.*

2 In this sacrament, Christ is not offered up to His Father; nor any real sacrifice made at all for remission of sins of the quick or dead;[b] but only a commemoration of that one offering up of Himself, by Himself, upon the cross, once for all: and a spiritual oblation of all possible praise unto God for the same:[c] so that the Popish sacrifice of the mass (as they call it) is most abominably injurious to Christ's one, only sacrifice, the alone propitiation for all the sins of His elect.[d]

[b] *Heb 9:22, 25-26,28.*

[c] *1 Cor 11:24-26; Matt 26:26-27.*

[d] *Heb 7:23-24,27; Heb 10:11-12,14,18.*

3 The Lord Jesus hath, in this ordinance, appointed His ministers to declare His word of institution to the people; to pray, and bless the elements of bread and wine, and thereby to set them apart from a common to a holy use; and to take and break the bread, to take the cup, and (they

communicating also themselves) to give both to the communicants;[e] but to none who are not then present in the congregation.[f]

[e] Matt 26:26-28 and Mark 14:22-24 and Luke 22:19-20 with 1 Cor 11:23-26.
[f] Acts 20:7; 1 Cor 11:20.

4 Private masses, or receiving this sacrament by a priest or any other alone;[g] as likewise, the denial of the cup to the people,[h] worshipping the elements, the lifting them up or carrying them about for adoration, and the reserving them for any pretended religious use; are all contrary to the nature of this sacrament, and to the institution of Christ.[i]

[g] 1 Cor 10:16.
[h] Mark 14:23; 1 Cor 11:25-29.
[i] Matt 15:9.

5 The outward elements in this sacrament, duly set apart to the uses ordained by Christ, have such relation to Him crucified, as that, truly, yet sacramentally only, they are sometimes called by the name of the things they represent, to wit, the body and blood of Christ;[k] albeit, in substance and nature they still remain truly and only bread and wine, as they were before.[l]

[k] Matt 26:26-28.
[l] 1 Cor 11:26-28; Matt 26:29.

6 That doctrine which maintains a change of the substance of bread and wine into the substance of Christ's body and blood (commonly called transubstantiation) by consecration of a priest, or by any other way, is repugnant, not to Scripture alone, but even to common sense and reason; overthroweth the nature of the sacrament, and hath been, and is the cause of manifold superstitions; yea, of gross idolatries.[m]

[m] Acts 3:21 with 1 Cor 11:24-26; Luke 24:6,39.

7 Worthy receivers outwardly partaking of the visible elements in this sacrament,[n] do then

[n] 1 Cor 11:28.

also, inwardly by faith, really and indeed, yet not carnally and corporally, but spiritually, receive and feed upon Christ crucified, and all benefits of His death: the body and blood of Christ being then, not corporally or carnally, in, with, or under the bread and wine; yet, as really, but spiritually, present to the faith of believers in that ordinance, as the elements themselves are to their outward senses.[o]

[o] 1 Cor 10:16.

8 Although ignorant and wicked men receive the outward elements in this sacrament; yet they receive not the thing signified thereby, but by their unworthy coming thereunto are guilty of the body and blood of the Lord to their own damnation. Wherefore, all ignorant and ungodly persons, as they are unfit to enjoy communion with Him, so are they unworthy of the Lord's table; and cannot, without great sin against Christ while they remain such, partake of these holy mysteries,[p] or be admitted thereunto.[q]

[p] 1 Cor 11:27-29; 2 Cor 6:14-16.
[q] 1 Cor 5:6-7,13; 2 Thess 3:6,14-15; Matt 7:6.

30
Of Church Censures

1 The Lord Jesus, as King and Head of His Church, hath therein appointed a government, in the hand of Church officers, distinct from the civil magistrate.[a]

[a] *Isa 9:6-7; 1 Tim 5:17; 1 Thess 5:12; Acts 20:17,28; Heb 13:7,17,24; 1 Cor 12:28; Matt 28:18-20.*

2 To these officers, the keys of the kingdom of heaven are committed; by virtue whereof, they have power respectively to retain, and remit sins; to shut that kingdom against the impenitent, both by the Word and censures; and to open it unto penitent sinners, by the ministry of the Gospel, and by absolution from censures, as occasion shall require.[b]

[b] *Matt 16:19; Matt 18:17-18; John 20:21-23; 2 Cor 2:6-8.*

3 Church censures are necessary, for the reclaiming and gaining of offending brethren, for deterring of others from the like offences, for purging out of that leaven which might infect the whole lump, for vindicating the honour of Christ, and the holy profession of the Gospel, and for preventing the wrath of God, which might justly fall upon the Church, if they should suffer His covenant and the seals thereof to be profaned by notorious and obstinate offenders.[c]

[c] *1 Cor chap 5; 1 Tim 5:20; Matt 7:6; 1 Tim 1:20; 1 Cor 11:27-34 with Jude 23.*

4 For the better attaining of these ends, the officers of the Church are to proceed by admonition; suspension from the sacrament of the Lord's Supper for a season; and by excommunication from the Church; according to the nature of the crime, and demerit of the person.[d]

[d] *1 Thess 5:12; 2 Thess 3:6,14-15; 1 Cor 5:4-5,13; Matt 18:17; Tit 3:10.*

31
Of Synods and Councils

[a]Acts 15:2,4,6.

1 For the better government, and further edification of the Church, there ought to be such assemblies as are commonly called synods or councils.[a]

[b]Isa 49:23; 1 Tim 2:1-2; 2 Chron 19:8-11; 2 Chron 29-30; Matt 2:4-5; Prov 11:14. [c]Acts 15:2,4, 22-23,25.

2 As magistrates may lawfully call a synod of ministers, and other fit persons, to consult and advise with, about matters of religion;[b] so, if magistrates be open enemies to the Church, the ministers of Christ of themselves, by virtue of their office, or they, with other fit persons, upon delegation from their Churches, may meet together in such assemblies.[c]

[d]Acts 15:15, 19,24,27-31; Acts 16:4; Matt 18:17-20.

3 It belongeth to synods and councils, ministerially to determine controversies of faith and cases of conscience, to set down rules and directions for the better ordering of the public worship of God, and government of His Church; to receive complaints in cases of maladministration, and authoritatively to determine the same: which decrees and determinations, if consonant to the Word of God, are to be received with reverence and submission; not only for their agreement with the Word, but also for the power whereby they are made, as being an ordinance of God appointed thereunto in His Word.[d]

4 All synods or councils, since the Apostles' times, whether general or particular, may err;

and many have erred. Therefore they are not to be made the rule of faith or practice; but to be used as a help in both.[e]

[e] *Eph 2:20; Acts 17:11; 1 Cor 2:5; 2 Cor 1:24.*

5 Synods and councils are to handle, or conclude, nothing, but that which is ecclesiastical: and are not to intermeddle with civil affairs which concern the commonwealth, unless by way of humble petition, in cases extraordinary; or by way of advice, for satisfaction of conscience, if they be thereunto required by the civil magistrate.[f]

[f] *Luke 12:13-14; John 18:36.*

32

Of the State of Men after Death, and of the Resurrection of the Dead

1 The bodies of men, after death, return to dust and see corruption.[a] But their souls (which neither die nor sleep) having an immortal subsistence, immediately return to God who gave them.[b] The souls of the righteous, being then made perfect in holiness, are received into the highest heavens, where they behold the face of God, in light and glory, waiting for the full redemption of their bodies.[c] And the souls of the wicked are cast into hell, where they remain in torments and utter darkness, reserved to the judgment of the great day.[d] Beside these two places, for souls separated from their bodies, the Scripture acknowledgeth none.

[a] *Gen 3:19; Acts 13:36.*
[b] *Luke 23:43; Eccl 12:7.*
[c] *Heb 12:23; 2 Cor 5:1,6,8; Phil 1:23 with Acts 3:21 and Eph 4:10.*
[d] *Luke 16:23-24; Acts 1:25; Jude 6-7; 1 Pet 3:19.*

2 At the last day, such as are found alive shall not die, but be changed:[e] and all the dead shall be raised up, with the selfsame bodies and none other, although with different qualities, which shall be united again to their souls for ever.[f]

[e] *1 Thess 4:17; 1 Cor 15:51-52.*
[f] *Job 19:26-27; 1 Cor 15:42-44.*

3 The bodies of the unjust shall, by the power of Christ, be raised to dishonour: the bodies of the just, by His Spirit, unto honour; and be made conformable to His own glorious body.[g]

[g] *Acts 24:15; John 5:28-29; 1 Cor 15:43; Phil 3:21.*

33
Of the Last Judgment

1 God hath appointed a day, wherein He will judge the world in righteousness, by Jesus Christ,[a] to whom all power and judgment is given of the Father;[b] in which day, not only the apostate angels shall be judged,[c] but likewise all persons that have lived upon earth shall appear before the tribunal of Christ, to give an account of their thoughts, words, and deeds; and to receive according to what they have done in the body, whether good or evil.[d]

[a] Acts 17:31.

[b] John 5:22,27.

[c] 1 Cor 6:3; Jude 6; 2 Pet 2:4.

[d] 2 Cor 5:10; Eccl 12:14; Rom 2:16; Rom 14:10,12; Matt 12:36-37.

2 The end of God's appointing this day is for the manifestation of the glory of His mercy, in the eternal salvation of the elect; and of His justice, in the damnation of the reprobate who are wicked and disobedient. For then shall the righteous go into everlasting life, and receive that fulness of joy and refreshing, which shall come from the presence of the Lord: but the wicked, who know not God, and obey not the Gospel of Jesus Christ, shall be cast into eternal torments, and be punished with everlasting destruction from the presence of the Lord, and from the glory of His power.[e]

[e] Matt 25:31-46; Rom 2:5-6; Rom 9:22-23; Matt 25:21; Acts 3:19; 2 Thess 1:7-10.

3 As Christ would have us to be certainly persuaded that there shall be a day of judgment, both to deter all men from sin, and for the greater consolation of the godly in their adversity;[f] so will He have that day unknown to men, that they may shake off all carnal security, and be always watchful, because they know not at what hour the Lord

[f] 2 Pet 3:11,14; 2 Cor 5:10-11; 2 Thess 1:5-7; Luke 21:27-28; Rom 8:23-25.

will come, and may be ever prepared to say, Come, Lord Jesus, come quickly, Amen.[g]

[g] Matt 24:36,42-44; Mark 13:35-37; Luke 12:35-36; Rev 22:20.

9 788196 076313

Printed at Repro India Ltd.